Aha! Grammar 2

Happy House

CoNTeNTs

Chapter 1 Nouns & Articles

Chapter 2 Pronouns

Chapter 3 Present Simple Tense

HOW TO USE

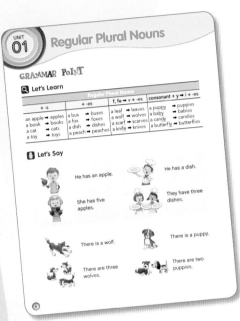

➲ Grammar Point

This section introduces basic grammar concepts with simple grammar charts in each unit. It also provides clear examples of how the target grammar rules are used along with illustrations.

Practice ⬅

This section provides various types of activities that allow learners to take a step-by-step approach to using the grammar rules. Learners can practice and learn the accurate use of grammar rules.

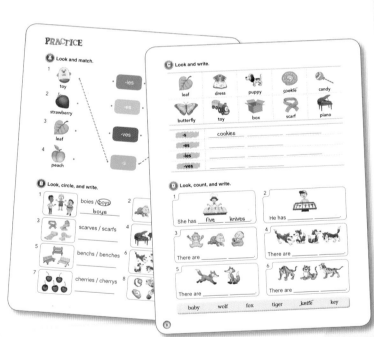

THIS BOOK

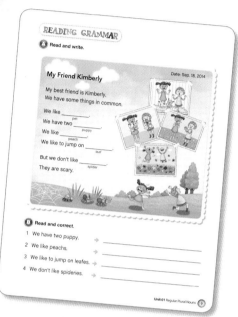

→ Reading Grammar

This section provides reading passages such as emails, journals, letters, and stories that help learners apply grammar rules in context and consolidate what they have studied. It also makes studying English grammar fun for learners.

Review ←

This section is found at the end of every chapter. It is designed to integrate grammar points that learners have studied from each unit. It can also assess and evaluate learners' understanding of the material.

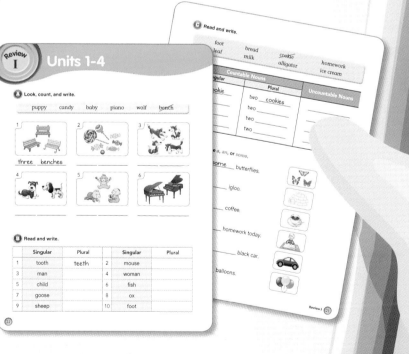

Regular Plural Nouns

GRAMMAR POINT

 Let's Learn

Regular Plural Nouns			
+ -s	+ -es	f, fe ➡ v + -es	consonant + y ➡ i + -es
an apple ➡ apples a book ➡ books a cat ➡ cats a toy ➡ toys	a bus ➡ buses a fox ➡ foxes a dish ➡ dishes a peach ➡ peaches	a lea_f_ ➡ leaves a wol_f_ ➡ wolves a scar_f_ ➡ scarves a kni_fe_ ➡ knives	a pup_py_ ➡ puppies a ba_by_ ➡ babies a can_dy_ ➡ candies a butterf_ly_ ➡ butterflies

🎙 **Let's Say**

 He has an apple.

 He has a dish.

 She has five apples.

 They have three dishes.

 There is a wolf.

 There is a puppy.

 There are three wolves.

 There are two puppies.

PRACTICE

A Look and match.

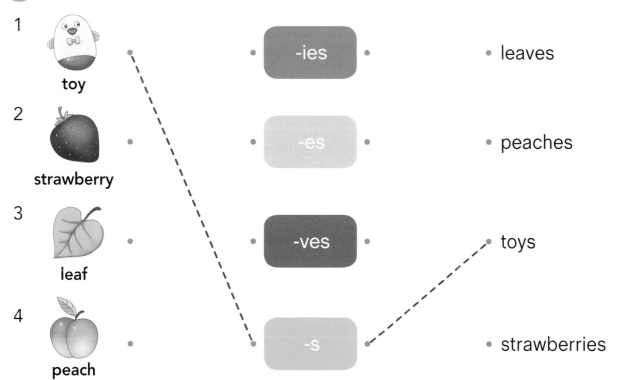

1 toy

2 strawberry

3 leaf

4 peach

-ies

-es

-ves

-s

· leaves

· peaches

· toys

· strawberries

B Look, circle, and write.

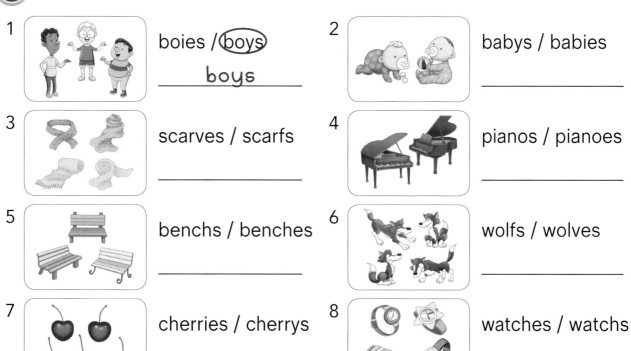

1 boies / (boys)

boys

2 babys / babies

_____

3 scarves / scarfs

_____

4 pianos / pianoes

_____

5 benchs / benches

_____

6 wolfs / wolves

_____

7 cherries / cherrys

_____

8 watches / watchs

_____

C Look and write.

leaf	dress	puppy	~~cookie~~	candy
butterfly	toy	box	scarf	piano

-s	cookies	_____	_____
-es	_____	_____	
-ies	_____	_____	_____
-ves	_____	_____	

D Look, count, and write.

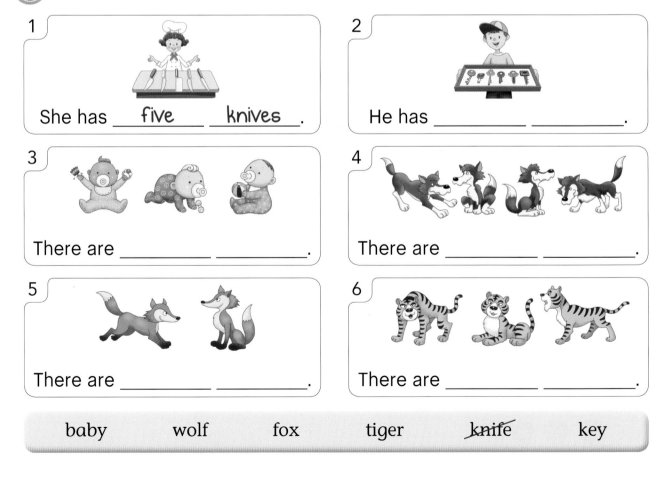

1 She has ___five___ ___knives___.

2 He has _____ _____.

3 There are _____ _____.

4 There are _____ _____.

5 There are _____ _____.

6 There are _____ _____.

baby   wolf   fox   tiger   ~~knife~~   key

READING GRAMMAR

A Read and write.

Date: Sep. 18, 2014

My Friend Kimberly

My best friend is Kimberly.
We have some things in common.

We like _____.
           pet
We have two _____.
           puppy
We like _____.
          peach
We like to jump on _____.
           leaf

But we don't like _____.
           spider
They are scary.

B Read and correct.

1 We have two puppy.   ⇒ _____

2 We like peachs.   ⇒ _____

3 We like to jump on leafes. ⇒ _____

4 We don't like spideries. ⇒ _____

Irregular Plural Nouns

GRAMMAR POINT

🔍 Let's Learn

Irregular Plural Nouns		
a man ➡ men	a goose ➡ geese	an ox ➡ oxen
a woman ➡ women	a sheep ➡ sheep	a child ➡ children
a foot ➡ feet	a deer ➡ deer	a person ➡ people
a tooth ➡ teeth	a fish ➡ fish	a mouse ➡ mice

🎤 Let's Say

 I have a goose.

 It has a fish.

 He has four geese.

 They have three fish.

 There is a child.

 There is an ox.

 There are three children.

 There are two oxen.

 There is a woman.

 There is a mouse.

 There are three women.

 There are five mice.

PRACTICE

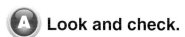

A Look and check.

1
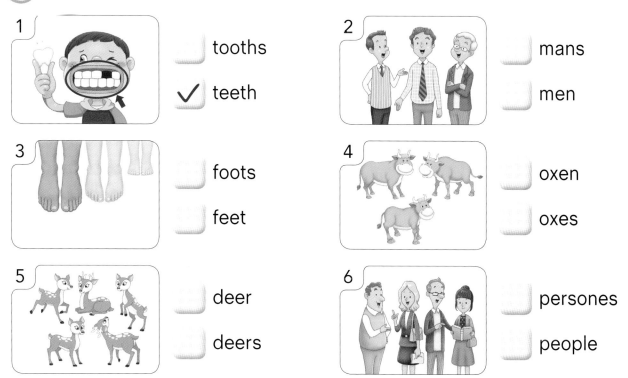

☐ tooths

✓ teeth

2

☐ mans

☐ men

3

☐ foots

☐ feet

4

☐ oxen

☐ oxes

5

☐ deer

☐ deers

6

☐ persones

☐ people

B Look, circle, and write.

1
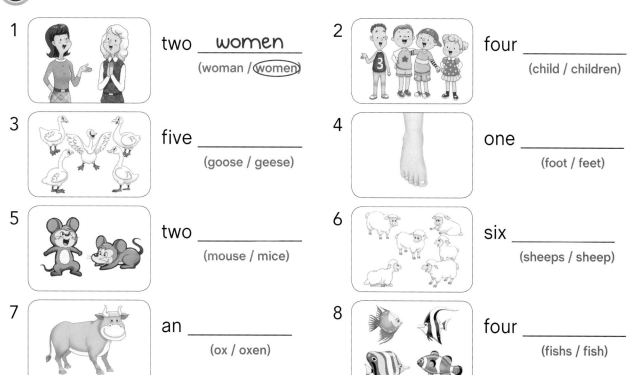

two __women__

(woman / <u>women</u>)

2

four _____

(child / children)

3

five _____

(goose / geese)

4

one _____

(foot / feet)

5

two _____

(mouse / mice)

6

six _____

(sheeps / sheep)

7

an _____

(ox / oxen)

8

four _____

(fishs / fish)

C **Write and match.**

1 a tooth → ten ___teeth___

2 a man → two _____

3 a mouse → five _____

4 a fish → three _____

5 an ox → four _____

D **Look, count, and write.**

1

He has ___four___ ___geese___ .

2

They have _____ _____ .

3

There are _____ _____ .

4

There are _____ _____ .

5

There are _____ _____ .

6

There are _____ _____ .

sheep	fish	child	deer	goose	woman

READING GRAMMAR

A Read and write.

My Family Has ...

My father has two _____.
ox

My mother has eight _____.
sheep

My grandmother has five _____.
goose

Oops! My family has three _____.
mouse

B Read, match, and write.

1 My father has • • two _____.

2 My mother has • • five _____.

3 My grandmother has • • three _____.

4 My family has • • eight _____.

Countable & Uncountable Nouns

GRAMMAR POINT

🔍 Let's Learn

Countable Nouns		Uncountable Nouns
Singular	**Plural**	
an elephant a box one wolf	two elephants five boxes two wolves	~~an~~ ice cream ~~a~~ water ~~one~~ cheese ~~two~~ sugar~~s~~

🎙 Let's Say

Countable Nouns		Uncountable Nouns

It is an orange.

They are oranges.

It is ice cream.

It is a candy.

They are candies.

It is water.

Is it a leaf?
Yes, It is.

Are they girls?
No, they aren't.

Is it butter?
No, it isn't.

PRACTICE

A Look and mark O or X.

1  five peaches O	2  two cheese ◯	3  four scarf ◯
4  money ◯	5  three juice ◯	6  an umbrella ◯

B Look and write.

Countable Nouns		Uncountable Nouns	
Singular	**Plural**		
1 ___a___ ___book___	2 _____ _____	3 _____ _____	4 _____ _____
5 _____ _____	6 _____ _____	7 _____ _____	8 _____ _____

milk   dress   igloo   bread   sheep   ~~book~~   sugar   butter

C **Look and write.**

1  **butter**

2 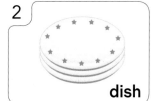 **dish**

3  **sandwich**

4  **bread**

5  **salt**

6  **orange**

7  **milk**

8  **watch**

1 ___It is butter.___

2 ___They are dishes.___

3 _____

4 _____

5 _____

6 _____

7 _____

8 _____

D **Look and write.**

1

2

3

__Is__ __it__ __an__ apple?
Yes, it is.

____ ____ cheese?
No, it isn't.

_____ _____ flowers?
Yes, they are.

4

5

6

____ ____ orange juice?
Yes, it is.

____ ____ ____ dress?
Yes, it is.

_____ _____ foxes?
No, they aren't.

READING GRAMMAR

A Read and write.

Our Dessert

We are at the restaurant.
After our meal, we want some dessert.

My dad wants _____.
coffee

My mom wants _____.
apple

I want _____.
ice cream

My brother wants _____,
juice

three _____,
sandwich

and ten _____.
cookie

Oh, brother. That's too much.

B Read, match, and write.

1 My dad wants •   •  _____.

2 My mom wants •   • _____.

3 I want •   • _____.

4 My brother wants •   •  _____.
_____.

UNIT 04 A/An/Some + Noun

GRAMMAR POINT

 Let's Learn

a / an + singular noun	some + plural noun	some + uncountable noun
an orange a watch a knife a candy	some oranges some watches some knives some candies	juice ➡ some juice butter ➡ some butter money ➡ some money homework ➡ some homework

Let's Say

There is a piano.

There is an orange.

There are some flowers.

There is some sugar.

There is some milk.

There is some butter.

Amy has a peach.
She has some bananas.

Tom has some bread.
He has some cheese.

PRACTICE

 A **Look and write using *a*, *an*, or *some*.**

1  2  3  4

some chocolate _____ _____ _____

5  6  7  8

_____ _____ _____ _____

| cheese | car | peach | sugar |
| umbrella | goose | ~~chocolate~~ | bus |

 B **Look and write *a*, *an*, or *some*.**

1  There is _____a_____ fox.

2  There are _____ eggs.

3  There is _____ ice cream.

4 There is _____ igloo.

5  There is _____ water.

6  There is _____ dress.

C Look and write using *a*, *an*, or *some*.

1 He has ___an___ ___apple___.

2 The cat has _____ _____.

3 They have _____ _____.

4 Amy has _____ _____.

5 The mouse has _____ _____.

cookie

~~apple~~

milk

dish

ice cream

D Look, read, and correct.

1 There is some breads.
   ⇒ There is some bread. _____

2 There are some pencil.
   ⇒ _____

3 There is a apple.
   ⇒ _____

4 He has some car.
   ⇒ _____

5 They have a homework.
   ⇒ _____

READING GRAMMAR

A Read and write *a*, *an*, or *some*.

Birthday Party List

Tomorrow is my brother Tom's birthday.
Mom and I are checking the list for his birthday party.

☑ We have _____ apples.

☑ We have _____ dishes.

☐ We need _____ birthday cake.

☐ We need _____ balloons.

☐ We need _____ orange juice.

☐ We need _____ present.

B Look and write using *a*, *an*, or *some*.

1   We have _____ _____.

2   We have _____ _____.

3   We need _____ _____.

4   We need _____ _____.

5   We need _____ _____.

6   We need _____ _____.

Units 1-4

 A **Look, count, and write.**

| puppy | candy | baby | piano | wolf | ~~bench~~ |

1

three benches

2

_____ _____

3

_____ _____

4

_____ _____

5

_____ _____

6

_____ _____

B **Read and write.**

	Singular	Plural		Singular	Plural
1	tooth	teeth	2	mouse	
3	man		4	woman	
5	child		6	fish	
7	goose		8	ox	
9	sheep		10	foot	

C Read and write.

cookie	~~homework~~	foot	bread
leaf	milk	alligator	ice cream

Countable Nouns		Uncountable Nouns
Singular	**Plural**	
a ___cookie___	two ___cookies___	___homework___
a _____	two _____	_____
a _____	two _____	_____
an _____	two _____	_____

D Look and write *a*, *an*, or *some*.

1 There are ___some___ butterflies.

2 There is _____ igloo.

3 There is _____ coffee.

4 Nick has _____ homework today.

5 My parents have _____ black car.

6 We have _____ balloons.

Possessive Adjectives

GRAMMAR POINT

🔍 Let's Learn

Subject Pronouns	Possessive Adjectives	
I	my	This is my toy. / My toy is red.
you	your	This is your toy. / Your toy is red.
he	his	This is his toy. / His toy is red.
she	her	This is her toy. / Her toy is red.
it	its	This is its toy. / Its toy is red.
we	our	This is our toy. / Our toy is red.
they	their	This is their toy. / Their toy is red.
Amy	Amy's	This is Amy's toy. / Amy's toy is red.

🎤 Let's Say

This is my camera.

These are your balloons.

Her house is big.

Whose backpack is it?
It is Lisa's backpack.

Whose bikes are they?
They are our bikes.

Whose bones are they?
They are its bones.

PRACTICE

A Look and circle.

1

Those are I (my) hats.

2

These are your I you bananas.

3

This is the cat I cat's fish.

4

That is we I our house.

B Look and write *his*, *her*, *its*, or *their*.

1 ___Her___ hat is yellow.

2 _____ jacket is green.

3 _____ tail is long.

4 _____ necks are long.

5 _____ backpack is blue.

6 _____ shoes are red.

7 _____ mouth is big.

8 _____ noses are long.

C Look, follow, and write.

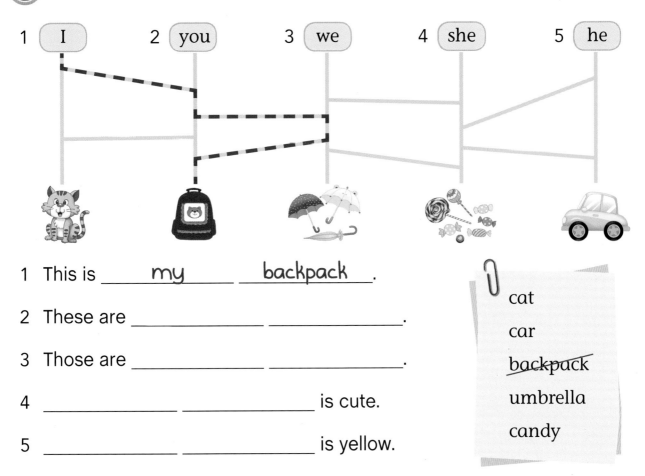

1 This is _____ my _____ _____ backpack _____ .

2 These are _____ _____ .

3 Those are _____ _____ .

4 _____ _____ is cute.

5 _____ _____ is yellow.

cat
car
~~backpack~~
umbrella
candy

D Look and write.

Whose skates are they?

They are _____ your _____ skates.

Whose ring is it?

It is _____ ring.

_____ umbrella is it?

It is _____ umbrella.

_____ crayons are they?

They are _____ crayons.

READING GRAMMAR

A Read and write.

About Our Items

These are _____ things.
I

_____ schoolbag is red.
I

_____ shoes are blue.
I

_____ watch is round.
I

These are _____ things.
He

_____ schoolbag is green.
He

_____ shoes are black.
He

_____ watch is square.
He

These are _____ things.
They

_____ schoolbags are white.
They

_____ shoes are yellow.
They

_____ watches are triangle.
They

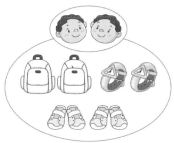

B Look, read, and write.

1 **I**

_____ watch is it?

It is _____ watch.

2 **he**

_____ schoolbag is it?

It is _____ schoolbag.

3  **they**

_____ shoes are they?

They are _____ shoes.

Possessive Pronouns

GRAMMAR PoINT

🔍 Let's Learn

Possessive Adjectives		Possessive Pronouns	
my	mine	This is <u>my pen</u>.	= This pen is mine.
your	yours	This is <u>your pen</u>.	= This pen is yours.
his	his	This is <u>his pen</u>.	= This pen is his.
her	hers	This is <u>her pen</u>.	= This pen is hers.
our	ours	This is <u>our pen</u>.	= This pen is ours.
their	theirs	This is <u>their pen</u>.	= This pen is theirs.
Amy	Amy's	This is <u>Amy's pen</u>.	= This pen is Amy's.

🎤 Let's Say

This is <u>my phone</u>.
= This phone is mine.

That is <u>your pen</u>.
= That pen is yours.

These are <u>our balloons</u>.
= These balloons are ours.

Whose glove is it?
It is his.

Whose cats are they?
They are hers.

Whose candies are they?
They are theirs.

PRACTICE

A **Read and check.**

1  That is my puppy. = That puppy is ✓ mine ☐ I.

2 This is your scarf. = This scarf is ☐ you ☐ yours.

3 That is his car. = That car is ☐ his ☐ he.

4 Those are her flowers. = Those flowers are ☐ her ☐ hers.

5 These are our books. = These books are ☐ ours ☐ we.

6 Those are their toys. = Those toys are ☐ their ☐ theirs.

B **Read, match, and write.**

1 This is her dress. •

2 These are his glasses. •

3 That is their puppy. •

4 This is my watch. •

5 That is your jacket. •

6 Those are our boots. •

• That puppy is _____.

• This watch is _____.

• That jacket is _____.

• This dress is _hers_.

• These glasses are _____.

• Those boots are _____.

C **Look and write.**

1

This is ___my___ computer.

→ This computer is ____mine____.

2

That is _____ car.

→ That car is _____.

3

Those are _____ shoes.

→ Those shoes are _____.

4

These are _____ notebooks.

→ These notebooks are _____.

5

Those are _____ candies.

→ Those candies are _____.

D **Look and write.**

1

Whose sneakers are they?

They are __their__ sneakers (= _theirs_).

2

Whose top is it?

It is _____ top (= _____).

3
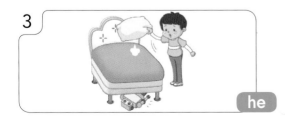

_____ robot is it?

It is _____ robot (= _____).

4

_____ mittens are they?

They are _____ mittens (= _____).

READING GRAMMAR

A Read and write.

It's Mine

Whose eraser is it?

Maybe it's _____.
(Jane)

Is this _____?
(you)

No, it's not _____.
(I)

It's not _____. Then it's _____.
(Jane) (I)

No, it's not _____.
It's _____.
(you) (we)

It's _____ now!
(he)

Oh, no!

B Look and write.

1. It's _____ eraser.
   = It's _____.

2. No, it's not _____ eraser.
   = No, it's not _____.

3. It's not _____ eraser.
   = It's not _____.

4. It's _____ eraser now!
   = It's _____ now!

UNIT 07

Object Pronouns (Singular)

GRAMMAR POINT

🔍 Let's Learn

Subject Pronouns	Object Pronouns (Singular)	
I	me	Tom likes me.
you	you	Tom likes you.
he	him	Tom likes him.
she	her	Tom likes her.
it	it	Tom likes it.

🎙 Let's Say

The puppies like me.

Your parents love you.

Tom helps her.

Sue likes her brother.
→ She likes him.

Sam likes the game.
→ He likes it.

Amy doesn't like her sister.
→ She doesn't like her.

Does he like his sister?
Yes, he likes her.

Do you like me?
Yes, I like you.

Do they like the bike?
Yes, they like it.

PRACTICE

A Look and match.

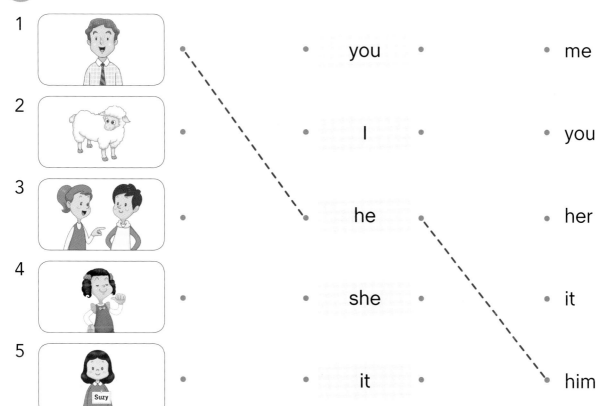

B Read, circle, and write.

1 Jimmy likes _____ me _____.

   (I /(me))

2 The puppies like _____.

   (she / her)

3 Your parents love _____.

   (you / your)

4 The student wants _____.

   (it / it's)

5 The police officer helps _____.

   (he / him)

6 My mother cooks _____.

   (it's / it)

C **Look, read, and change.**

1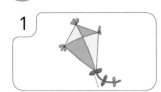

John wants a kite.

➡ ___He___ wants ___it___.

2

My grandmother loves my sister.

➡ _____ loves _____.

3

The girls like Peter.

➡ _____ like _____.

4

Mr. Brown knows Kelly.

➡ _____ knows _____.

5

The cat has a cookie.

➡ _____ has _____.

D **Look and write.**

1

Do you like me?

No, I don't like ___you___.

2

Does he like the game?

Yes, he likes _____.

3

Does she like her sister?

No, she doesn't like _____.

4

Do the students like their teacher?

Yes, they like _____.

READING GRAMMAR

A Read and write.

My Favorite Book: *Peter Pan*

My favorite book is *Peter Pan*.

I like _____ very much.
__it__

Peter Pan meets Wendy.

He likes _____.
__she__

Wendy likes _____, too.
__he__

They become friends.

They fly to Neverland.

I want Peter Pan to come to

see _____ in my dream.
__I__

B Look, read, and change.

1   I like the book *Peter Pan*.

→ I like _____.

2 Peter Pan likes Wendy.

→ Peter Pan likes _____.

3   Wendy likes Peter Pan, too.

→ Wendy likes _____, too.

4 I want Peter Pan to come to see _____ in my dream.

Object Pronouns (Plural)

GRAMMAR POINT

🔍 Let's Learn

Subject Pronouns	Object Pronouns (Plural)	
we	us	Tom likes us.
you	you	Tom likes you.
they	them	Tom likes them.

🎙 Let's Say

Your father loves you.

Sally has them.

Tom knows my brother and me.
→ He knows us.

Amy wants the shoes.
→ She wants them.

Does she like the sandwiches?
Yes, she likes them.

Do the horses like the girls?
Yes, they like them.

PRACTICE

A Look and mark O or X.

1

He has their. ✗

2

My mother loves us. ◯

3

The puppies like your. ◯

4

The horses like we. ◯

5

Lisa eats them. ◯

6

Your father loves you. ◯

B Look, circle, and write.

1

He wears __them__.

(they / ⓣhem)

2

My sister knows _____.

(you / your)

3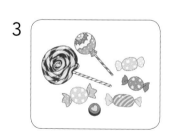

The children love _____.

(them / their)

4

He likes _____.

(our / us)

5

The puppies like _____.

(your / you)

6

The students like _____.

(us / we)

C Look, read, and change.

1  Kelly wants sandwiches.
→ ___She___ wants ___them___ .

2  Your father likes you and your brother.
→ _____ likes _____ .

3  Our mother loves my sister and me.
→ _____ loves _____ .

4  The twins like the puppies.
→ _____ like _____ .

5  Our grandparents love my brother and me.
→ _____ love _____ .

D Look, read, and correct.

1  Sally has their. → ___them___

2  Our mother loves we. → _____

3  My sister knows your. → _____

4  The students like our. → _____

READING GRAMMAR

I Miss You So Much

Dear Grandma and Grandpa,

How are you?

Thank you for the scarf and the mittens.

I like _____ very much.

they

I wear _____ outside.

they

Dad, Mom, and I are fine.

Can you come to see _____?

we

I miss _____ so much.

you

Love,

Amy

B Look, read, and change.

1

I like <u>the scarf and the mittens.</u>
→ I like _____.

2

Can you come to see <u>Dad, Mom, and me</u>?
→ Can you come to see _____.

3

I miss <u>you and Grandpa</u>.
→ I miss _____.

A **Look and write.**

1
I

This is ___my___ camera.

2
we

That is _____ house.

3
Tony

_____ backpack is blue.

4
she

Whose cats are they?

They are _____ _____.

5
he

_____ robot is it?

It is _____ _____.

6
they

_____ candies are they?

They are _____ _____.

B **Read, match, and write.**

1 This is my eraser.

2 That is our house.

3 Those are her boots.

4 That is your bike.

5 These are his bats.

6 These are their hats.

• That bike is _____.

• Those boots are _____.

• This eraser is ___mine___.

• These bats are _____.

• That house is _____.

• These hats are _____.

hers   ours   theirs   his   yours   ~~mine~~

C Look, read, and correct.

1. Our grandparents love <u>we</u>. ➡ _____ us _____

2. She wants <u>they</u>. ➡ _____

3. Your father loves <u>your</u>. ➡ _____

4. Jenny doesn't like <u>he</u>. ➡ _____

5. Tom helps <u>she</u>. ➡ _____

6. The puppies like <u>I</u>. ➡ _____

D Read and write.

	Subject Pronouns	Possessive Adjectives	Possessive Pronouns	Object Pronouns
1	I			me
2	you		yours	
3	he	his		
4	she		hers	
5	it		–	
6	we			us
7	they		theirs	

Present Simple (Affirmatives)

GRAMMAR POINT

🔍 Let's Learn

Present Simple (Affirmatives)			
I You We They	drink milk.	He She It Jane	drinks milk.

Regular Verbs		Irregular Verbs
+ -s	drink ➡ drinks, play ➡ plays	have ➡ has
+ -es	watch ➡ watches, brush ➡ brushes	go ➡ goes
y ➡ i + -es	study ➡ studies, cry ➡ cries	do ➡ does

🎙 Let's Say

I play the violin.
/ She plays the violin.

We watch TV.
/ The cat watches TV.

They study English.
/ She studies English.

You have a cat.
/ She has a cat.

They go to school.
/ He goes to school.

We do our homework.
/ Tom does his homework.

PRACTICE

A Look and mark O or X.

1
I drinks milk. X

2
We watch TV. ○

3
They flies kites. ○

4
She have apples. ○

5
The cat eats a fish. ○

6
He goes to school. ○

B Read, circle, and write.

1 She _____brushes_____ her hair.
(brush / ⃝brushes⃝)

2 He _____ his hands.
(wash / washes)

3 The babies _____ every night.
(cry / cries)

4 The alligator _____ in the river.
(live / lives)

5 You _____ to bed at 9:30.
(go / goes)

6 It _____ cheese every day.
(eat / eats)

7 I _____ my homework.
(do / does)

C **Look and write.**

	In the Morning	In the Afternoon
I	play the violin	clean the house
Sally	study English	go swimming
My father	read books	watch TV

1 I _____play the violin_____ in the morning.

2 Sally _____ in the morning.

3 My father _____ in the morning.

4 I _____ in the afternoon.

5 Sally _____ in the afternoon.

6 My father _____ in the afternoon.

D **Check and write.**

		study	play	watch	do	wash
1	Amy __watches__ TV after school.			✓		
2	We _____ English every day.					
3	He _____ his homework.					
4	My brother _____ the violin.					
5	They _____ their feet.					

READING GRAMMAR

 A **Read, look, and write.**

After-School Activities

I _____ swimming on Monday.

I _____ Chinese on Wednesday.

I _____ books on Friday.

My sister _____ tennis on Tuesday.

She _____ Chinese on Wednesday.

She _____ a DVD on Thursday.

She _____ to an art class on Friday.

| play |
| read |
| study |
| watch |
| go |

	Monday	Tuesday	Wednesday	Thursday	Friday
I					
My sister					

B **Read and write.**

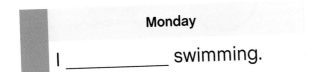

Monday

I _____ swimming.

Tuesday

My sister _____ tennis.

Wednesday

My sister and I _____ Chinese.

Thursday

My sister _____ a DVD.

Friday

• I _____ books.

• My sister _____ to an art class.

Present Simple (Negatives)

GRAMMAR PoINT

Q Let's Learn

Present Simple (Negatives)					
I You We They	don't	drink wash study have go	He She It Jane	doesn't	drink wash study have go

* don't = do not / doesn't = does not

🎙 Let's Say

I play the violin.
I don't play the piano.

He drinks some juice.
He doesn't drink some water.

We wash our faces.
We don't wash our feet.

She studies math.
She doesn't study English.

They go to the swimming pool.
They don't go to the park.

It has a bone.
It doesn't have a toy.

PRACTICE

A Look and circle.

1

He ⟨doesn't⟩ don't wash his face.

2

I don't I doesn't study math.

3

We don't I doesn't ride bikes.

4

It don't I doesn't climb a tree.

5

They doesn't I don't watch TV.

6

She don't I doesn't play the piano.

B Read and write.

1 She finishes her homework. ⟷ She __doesn't__ __finish__ her homework.

2 We have a cat. ⟷ We _____ _____ a cat.

3 He drinks coffee at night. ⟷ He _____ _____ coffee at night.

4 He does his homework. ⟷ He _____ _____ his homework.

5 The baby cries at night. ⟷ The baby _____ _____ at night.

6 They cook spaghetti. ⟷ They _____ _____ spaghetti.

C **Read and write the negatives.**

1 My grandparents ___don't___ ___watch___ TV.

2 The dog _____ _____ at night.

3 She _____ _____ her hair.

4 He _____ _____ a bike every day.

5 We _____ _____ our homework.

6 My father _____ _____ breakfast.

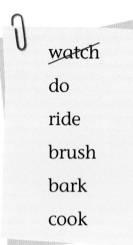

watch

do

ride

brush

bark

cook

D **Look and write.**

1

study

Jim ___studies___ English.
He ___doesn't___ ___study___ Chinese.

2

drink

The children _____ milk.
They _____ _____ coffee.

3

play

Jack and I _____ baseball.
We _____ _____ tennis.

4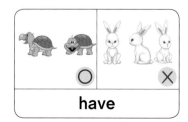

have

My mother _____ turtles.
She _____ _____ rabbits.

READING GRAMMAR

 A **Read and write.**

My Family Album

They are my grandparents.

They _____ books at night.
        read

They _____ TV at night.
              watch

This is my baby sister.

She _____ all day.
        smile

She _____.
           cry

This is my dad.

He _____ to work on foot.
       go

He _____ a car to work.
            drive

They are my mom and me.

We _____ a walk in the afternoon.
       take

We _____ in the afternoon.
           sleep

B **Look and write.**

1 My grandparents _____ _____ TV at night.

2 My baby sister _____ _____.

3 My dad _____ _____ a car to work.

4 My mom and I _____ _____ in the afternoon.

Present Simple (Yes / No Questions)

GRAMMAR POINT

🔍 Let's Learn

Question	Answer	
Do — I / you / we / you / they — sleep?	Yes, — you / I / you / we / they — do.	No, — you / I / you / we / they — don't.
Does — he / she / it — sleep?	Yes, — he / she / it — does.	No, — he / she / it — doesn't.

🎤 Let's Say

Do you teach English?
No, I don't.

Do they eat breakfast?
Yes, they do.

Do we walk to school?
No, you don't.

Does she drink milk?
No, she doesn't.

Does he study math?
Yes, he does.

Does it sleep at night?
No, it doesn't.

PRACTICE

A **Read and circle.**

1 (Do) I Does   you drink tea?
   Yes, I (do) I does   .

2   Do I Does   he fly a kite?
   No, he   don't I doesn't   .

3   Do I Does   it eat fish?
   Yes, it   do I does   .

4   Do I Does   they study English?
   No, they   don't I doesn't   .

5   Do I Does   she watch TV?
   Yes, she   do I does   .

6   Do I Does   we go to the park?
   No, you   don't I doesn't   .

B **Look, write, and check.**

1

   ___Does___ Mr. Jackson teach math?
   ✓ No, he doesn't.   Yes, he does.

2

   _____ you do your homework?
   No, we don't.   Yes, we do.

3

   _____ the giraffe eat leaves?
   Yes, it does.   No, it doesn't.

4

   _____ they watch TV?
   Yes, they do.   No, they don't.

C Look, follow, and write.

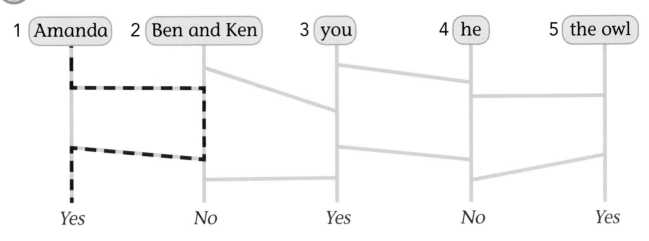

1 Amanda 2 Ben and Ken 3 you 4 he 5 the owl

Yes   No   Yes   No   Yes

1 ____Does____ Amanda fly a kite? __Yes__ , __she__ __does__ .

2 _____ Ben and Ken swim? _____ , _____ _____ .

3 _____ you wash your hands? _____ , _____ _____ .

4 _____ he go to school? _____ , _____ _____ .

5 _____ the owl sleep at night? _____ , _____ _____ .

D Read and write the question.

1 He goes to the park.

→ __Does he go to the park__ ? Yes, he does.

2 They walk to school.

→ _____ ? No, they don't.

3 Amy studies math.

→ _____ ? Yes, she does.

4 The cat chases a mouse.

→ _____ ? No, it doesn't.

5 The giraffes eat leaves.

→ _____ ? Yes, they do.

52

READING GRAMMAR

A Read and unscramble.

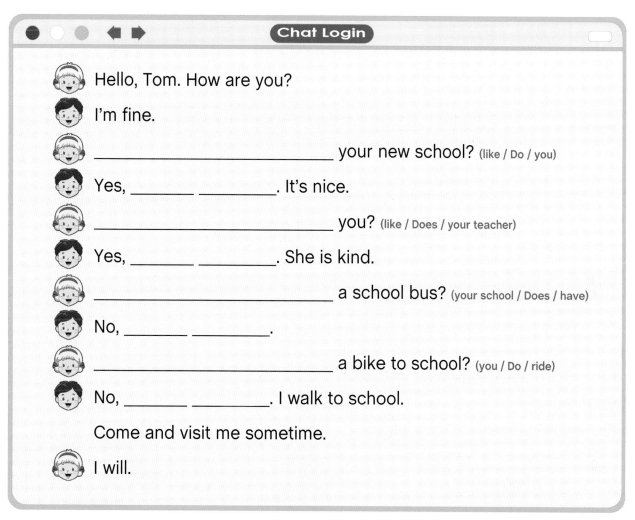

Chat Login

Hello, Tom. How are you?

I'm fine.

_____ your new school? (like / Do / you)

Yes, _____ _____. It's nice.

_____ you? (like / Does / your teacher)

Yes, _____ _____. She is kind.

_____ a school bus? (your school / Does / have)

No, _____ _____.

_____ a bike to school? (you / Do / ride)

No, _____ _____. I walk to school.

Come and visit me sometime.

I will.

B Look and write.

1.  _____ Tom like his new school?

   _____, _____ _____.

2.  _____ Tom's teacher like him?

   _____, _____ _____.

3. _____ Tom ride a bike to school?

   _____, _____ _____.

Simple Present (What Questions)

GRAMMAR PoINT

🔍 Let's Learn

Question			Answer		
What do	I you we you they	do?	You I You We They	drink	milk.
What does	he she it	do?	He She It	drinks	milk.

🎤 Let's Say

What do you do?
I brush my teeth.

What does she do?
She cooks dinner.

What does the cat do?
It chases a mouse.

What do they do?
They read newspapers.

What does he do?
He studies math.

What does the giraffe do?
It eats leaves.

PRACTICE

A Read and circle.

1 What do I(does) he do?

He fly I(flies) a kite.

2 What do I does it do?

It catch I catches a mouse.

3 What do I does they do?

They washes I wash their feet.

4 What do I does she do?

She drink I drinks some water.

5 What do I does you do?

I watches I watch TV.

6 What do I does I do?

You ride I rides a bike.

B Look and write.

1  study

What does he do?

He ___studies___ ___English___ .

2  read

What do they do?

They _____ _____ .

3  eat

What does the dog do?

It _____ _____ .

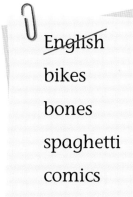

~~English~~

bikes

bones

spaghetti

comics

4  cook

What does your mother do?

She _____ _____ .

5  ride

What do you do?

We _____ _____ .

C Read, look, and write the question.

1 <u>What do you do in the morning</u> ?

   I swim in the morning.

2 _____ ?

   I play the flute in the afternoon.

3 _____ ?

   I watch TV in the evening.

4 _____ ?

   Jenny cleans her room in the morning.

5 _____ ?

   Jenny studies English in the afternoon.

6 _____ ?

   Jenny does her homework in the evening.

	I	Jenny
Morning		
Afternoon		English ABC
Evening		Homework

D Look and write.

	climb	brush	drive	do
Diana				✓
Tom and Sue		✓		
Mr. Baker			✓	
The monkey	✓			

1 <u>What</u> <u>does</u> Diana do? She <u>does</u> her homework.

2 _____ _____ Tom and Sue do? They _____ their teeth.

3 _____ _____ Mr. Baker do? He _____ a car.

4 _____ _____ the monkey do? It _____ a tree.

READING GRAMMAR

A Read and write.

Lynn Carey's Daily Life

A TV reporter is interviewing Lynn Carey, a pop idol.

Hello. Thank you very much for speaking with us.

It's my pleasure.

_____ _____ _____ do in the morning?

I _____ a walk with my dog.

_____ _____ _____ do in the afternoon?

I _____ songs and _____ music.

_____ _____ _____ do in the evening?

I _____ books all night.

_____ _____ _____ read all night?

I _____ comics. They are so much fun!

| listen to | take | sing | read |

B Read and write.

1 _____ _____ Lynn _____ in the morning?

She _____ a walk with her dog.

2 _____ _____ Lynn _____ in the afternoon?

She _____ songs and _____ music.

3 _____ _____ Lynn _____ in the evening?

She _____ books all night.

A Read and write.

1 run ➡ She ___runs___.

2 drink ➡ He _____.

3 go ➡ We _____.

4 study ➡ She _____.

5 brush ➡ They _____.

6 do ➡ You _____.

7 finish ➡ It _____.

8 fly ➡ The bird _____.

9 wash ➡ I _____.

10 cook ➡ My mother _____.

B Look and write.

1

He __doesn't__ __study__ math.

2

They _____ _____ basketball.

3

My father _____ _____ a car.

4

The baby _____ _____ at night.

5

We _____ _____ TV.

6

The monkeys _____ _____ the trees.

C Look and write.

1
sleep

_____Does_____ the owl _____sleep_____ at night?

No, ___it___ ___doesn't___.

2
brush

_____ he _____ his teeth?

Yes, _____ _____.

3
do

_____ they _____ their homework?

No, _____ _____.

4
teach

_____ she _____ math?

Yes, _____ _____.

D Read, choose, and write.

1 What does he do?

__He rides a bike__.

2 What do you do?

_____

3 _____

They watch TV.

4 _____

She studies English.

• What does she do?   • ~~He rides a bike.~~
• What do they do?   • I do my homework.

Present Continuous (Affirmatives)

GRAMMAR POINT

🔍 Let's Learn

Present Continuous (Affirmatives)		
I	am	sleeping.
You	are	sleeping.
He / She / It	is	sleeping.
We / You / They	are	sleeping.

+ -ing	~e + -ing	double consonant + -ing
play ➡ playing	make ➡ making	run ➡ running
sing ➡ singing	dance ➡ dancing	swim ➡ swimming
walk ➡ walking	drive ➡ driving	hit ➡ hitting

🎙️ Let's Say

I am singing.

The cat is sleeping.

You are dancing.

He is driving a car.

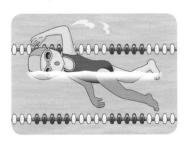

She is swimming.

We are running.

PRACTICE

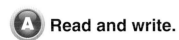

A Read and write.

hop	go	make	stand	sit	write
swim	run	dance	ride	sing	watch

+ -ing	~e~ + -ing	double consonant + -ing
going	_____	_____
_____	_____	_____
_____	_____	_____
_____	_____	_____

B Look, circle, and write.

1

It _____is_____ snowing.
(are / (is))

2

They _____ walking.
(am / are)

3

He _____ cutting.
(am / is)

4

I _____ dancing.
(am / are)

5

You _____ writing.
(are / is)

6

We _____ swimming.
(are / is)

C Look and write.

1
ride

I ____am____ ____riding____ a bike.

2
play

They _____ _____ basketball.

3
write

She _____ _____ an email.

4
climb

The monkeys _____ _____ the trees.

5
hit

David _____ _____ a ball.

D Look, write, and put the correct number.

1 He ____is____ ____driving____ a car.

2 The children _____ _____ some paper.

3 The giraffe _____ _____ leaves.

4 My mother _____ _____ dinner.

cook

~~drive~~

eat

cut

1

READING GRAMMAR

A **Read and write.**

My Field Trip to the Zoo

I am at the zoo.

Look at the monkeys.
They are _____ a tree.
climb

Look at the dolphin.
It is _____ in the water.
jump

Look at the zebras.
They are _____.
run

Look at the boy.
He is _____ an elephant.
ride
How exciting!

B **Look, read, and write.**

1  The monkeys _____ _____ a tree.

2  The dolphin _____ _____ in the water.

3 The zebras _____ _____.

4 The boy _____ _____ an elephant.

Present Continuous (Negatives)

GRAMMAR POINT

🔍 Let's Learn

Present Continuous (Negatives)		
I	am not (= 'm not)	swimming.
You	are not (= aren't)	swimming.
He / She / It	is not (= isn't)	swimming.
We / You / They	are not (= aren't)	swimming.

🎤 Let's Say

I'm not sleeping.
I am walking.

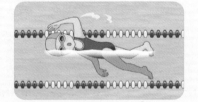

I'm not writing.
I am swimming.

You aren't studying.
You are dancing.

She isn't cooking.
She is cleaning.

He isn't running.
He is riding a bike.

It isn't raining.
It is snowing.

We aren't sitting.
We are running.

They aren't dancing.
They are singing.

The babies aren't smiling.
They are crying.

PRACTICE

A **Read and circle.**

1 I **('m not)** / isn't playing the cello.

2 She aren't / isn't hitting.

3 He aren't / isn't writing.

4 We 'm not / aren't standing.

5 They aren't / isn't chatting.

6 You isn't / aren't drinking.

7 I 'm not / isn't dancing.

8 It isn't / aren't swimming.

B **Look and write.**

1
ride

We __aren't__ __riding__ our bikes.
We are singing.

2
sit

I ____ ____ _____ on a bench.
I am hitting a ball.

3
draw

He _____ _____ a picture.
He is cutting some paper.

4
brush

Lynn _____ _____ her teeth.
She is reading comic books.

5
swim

The penguins _____ _____.
They are walking.

C **Look, read, and write.**

1  2  3  4

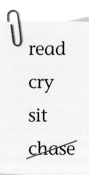

1 The cat __isn't__ __chasing__ a mouse.

2 The babies _____ _____ at night.

3 My father _____ _____ a newspaper.

4 She _____ _____ on the bench.

read

cry

sit

~~chase~~

D **Look and write.**

1

⊗ sing
◎ dance

➡ You ___aren't singing___.
➡ You ___are dancing___.

2

⊗ write
◎ cut

➡ We _____.
➡ We _____.

3

⊗ walk
◎ swim

➡ The penguin _____.
➡ It _____.

4

⊗ stand
◎ sit

➡ I _____.
➡ I _____.

5

⊗ study
◎ run

➡ They _____.
➡ They _____.

6

⊗ clean
◎ cook

➡ My mother _____.
➡ She _____.

READING GRAMMAR

 A **Read and write.**

They Aren't Sleeping

It is a dark night.
People are sleeping. But ...

The mice _____.
sleep

They _____.
run

The owl _____.
sleep

It _____.
hunt

The bats _____.
sleep

They _____.
fly

The dog _____.
sleep

It _____.
bark

B **Read, write, and match.**

1 The mice _____ sleeping. •

2 The owl _____ sleeping. •

3 The bats _____ sleeping. •

4 The dog _____ sleeping. •

 • They _____ _____.

 • They _____ _____.

• It _____ _____.

 • It _____ _____.

Present Continuous (Yes / No Questions)

GRAMMAR PoINT

🔍 Let's Learn

Question	Answer
Am I running?	Yes, you are. / No, you aren't.
Are you running?	Yes, I am. / No, I'm not.
Is he running?	Yes, he is. / No, he isn't.
Is she running?	Yes, she is. / No, she isn't.
Is it running?	Yes, it is. / No, it isn't.
Are we running?	Yes, you are. / No, you aren't.
Are you running?	Yes, we are. / No, we aren't.
Are they running?	Yes, they are. / No, they aren't.

🎙 Let's Say

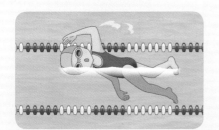

Are you swimming?
Yes, I am.

Is she drawing?
Yes, she is.

Is the monkey climbing?
No, it isn't.

Are they running?
Yes, they are.

Are you studying?
No, we aren't.

Are the penguins sleeping?
No, they aren't.

PRACTICE

A Read and circle.

1   Am I **Are** I Is you drinking?

2   Am I Are I Is he driving?

3   Am I Are I Is they swimming?

4   Am I Are I Is it flying?

5   Am I Are I Is she sitting?

6   Am I Are I Is the cat sleeping?

7   Am I Are I Is I walking?

8   Am I Are I Is we drawing?

B Look, circle, and write.

1      Is he studying math? _____ Yes, he is. _____
(**Yes, he is.** / No, he isn't.)

2      Is she riding a bike? _____
(Yes, she is. / No, she isn't.)

3      Are they crying? _____
(Yes, they are. / No, they aren't.)

4      Are you watching TV? _____
(No, we aren't. / Yes, we are.)

5      Is the dog barking? _____
(No, it isn't. / Yes, it is.)

6      Are the penguins walking? _____
(Yes, they are. / No, they aren't.)

C **Read and write.**

1 she / sing   ___Is she singing___ ? No, she isn't.

2 you / draw   _____? Yes, I am.

3 they / swim   _____? No, they aren't.

4 the dog / bark   _____? Yes, it is.

5 he / stand   _____? Yes, he is.

6 the children / run   _____? No, they aren't.

D **Read, look, and write.**

1 Peter Pan is running.

   ➡ ___Is Peter Pan running___ ?
     ___No, he isn't___ .

2 The seven dwarfs are working.

   ➡ _____?
     _____.

3 Snow White is drinking some water.

   ➡ _____?
     _____.

4 The ducklings are swimming.

   ➡ _____?
     _____.

READING GRAMMAR

A Read and write.

A Scary Movie

_____ the vampires
_____?
walk

Yes, _____ _____.

_____ the witch
_____?
fly

Yes, _____ _____.

_____ the ghosts
_____?
jump

Yes, _____ _____.
But there's no ghost now.

Boo!

Yikes!

B Look, read, and correct.

1 <u>Is the vampires walking? Yes, they are.</u>

➡ _____

2 <u>Is the witch fly? Yes, she is.</u>

➡ _____

3 <u>Are the ghosts jump? Yes, they are.</u>

➡ _____

UNIT 16

Present Continuous (Wh- Questions)

GRAMMAR POINT

🔍 Let's Learn

What Question				Answer			
What	am	I		You		are	
What	are	you	doing?	I		am	drinking.
What	is	he / she / it		He / She / It		is	
What	are	we / you / they		You / We / They		are	
Who Question				**Answer**			
Who		is	running?	Amy		is	running.
				The children		are	running.

🎙 Let's Say

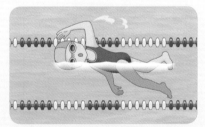

What are you doing?
I am swimming.

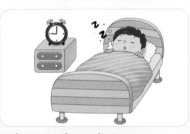

What is he doing?
He is sleeping.

What are the birds doing?
They are sitting.

Who is flying?
Peter Pan is flying.

Who is dancing?
Amy is dancing.

Who is walking?
The penguins are walking.

PRACTICE

A Read, circle, and write.

1 ___What___ is she doing?   She ___is___ swimming.
   (Who /(What))

2 _____ is sleeping?   My brother _____ sleeping.
   (Who / What)

3 _____ are they doing?   They _____ writing.
   (Who / What)

4 _____ is working?   The seven dwarfs _____ working.
   (Who / What)

5 _____ is climbing?   The monkey _____ climbing.
   (Who / What)

6 _____ are you doing?   I _____ listening to music.
   (Who / What)

B Look and write.

1

   ___What___ is the cat doing?
   It ___is___ ___chasing___ a mouse.

2

   _____ are they doing?
   They _____ _____ their teeth.

3

   _____ is Snow White doing?
   She _____ _____ an apple.

   write
   ~~chase~~
   brush
   eat

4

   _____ are you doing?
   I _____ _____ an email.

C **Read, follow, and write.**

1 __Who__ is singing?   ___My friends___ are singing.

2 _____ is swimming?   _____ are swimming.

3 _____ is dancing?   _____ is dancing.

4 _____ is climbing?   _____ is climbing.

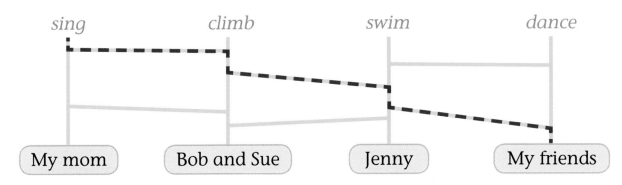

sing   *climb*   *swim*   *dance*

| My mom | Bob and Sue | Jenny | My friends |

D **Look and write.**

1 What ___is Peter doing___?   He is riding a bike.

2 What _____?   They are playing on the seesaw.

3 What _____?   It is digging a hole.

4 Who is building a sandcastle?   _____

5 Who is climbing a tree?   _____

READING GRAMMAR

A **Read and write.**

What Are You Doing?

John and his mother are talking on the phone.

Hello, John. What _____ _____ _____?

Oh... I'm reading a book.

_____ _____ Amy _____?

Ah... She is studying.

But I can hear some sounds.
Who _____ _____ a computer game?

Sorry, Mom. I am playing a computer game.

Then _____ _____ _____?

Amy is snoring.

B **Look, read, and write.**

1   _____ _____ John and his mother _____?

     They _____ _____ on the phone.

2   _____ _____ John _____?

     He _____ _____ a computer game.

3   _____ _____ snoring?

     Amy _____ _____.

Units 13-16

A Look and write.

| snow | sing | run | dance | ~~cook~~ | sleep |

1

She __is__ __cooking__.

2

It _____ _____.

3

I _____ _____.

4

They _____ _____.

5

You _____ _____.

6

We _____ _____.

B Read and write.

1 They / not / ride → They aren't riding.

2 The babies / not / cry → _____

3 We / not / dance → _____

4 I / not / stand → _____

5 My father / not / brush → _____

6 The frog / not / swim → _____

7 You / not / write → _____

C Look and write.

1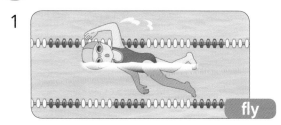
fly

___Is___ she __flying__ a kite?
___No__ , __she___ __isn't___ .

2
cut

_____ they _____ some paper?
_____ , _____ _____ .

3
walk

_____ the penguins _____ ?
_____ , _____ _____ .

4
ride

_____ he _____ a bike?
_____ , _____ _____ .

D Read, choose, and write.

1 Who is reading a book?

Sam is reading a book.

2 _____

I am writing a letter.

3 Who is swimming?

_____

4 What is Lucy doing?

_____

- Who is reading a book?
- What are you doing?
- She is building a sandcastle.
- The penguins are swimming.

UNIT 17 Comparatives

GRAMMAR POINT

🔍 Let's Learn

+ -er	long ➡ longer, fast ➡ faster, short ➡ shorter
+ -r	large ➡ larger, nice ➡ nicer, cute ➡ cuter
y ➡ i + -er	pretty ➡ prettier, happy ➡ happier, easy ➡ easier
double consonant + -er	big ➡ bigger, hot ➡ hotter, fat ➡ fatter
more + adjective	beautiful ➡ more beautiful, expensive ➡ more expensive, difficult ➡ more difficult

🎙 Let's Say

The kangaroo is faster than the turtle.

The elephant is larger than the cat.

The blouse is dirtier than the skirt.

Summer is hotter than spring.

The computer is more expensive than the camera.

Camping is more interesting than fishing.

PRACTICE

A Read and write.

1 fast → __faster__

2 strong → _____

3 fat → _____

4 heavy → _____

5 easy → _____

6 large → _____

7 beautiful → _____

8 cute → _____

9 expensive → _____

10 hot → _____

B Look and write.

1

The elephant is ___bigger___ than the mouse.

big

2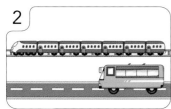

The train is _____ than the bus.

long

3

The pink hat is _____ than the yellow hat.

pretty

4

China is _____ than Japan.

large

5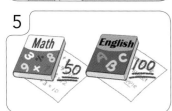

Math is _____ than English.

difficult

C **Look and write.**

~~slow~~   strong   fat   tall   expensive   large

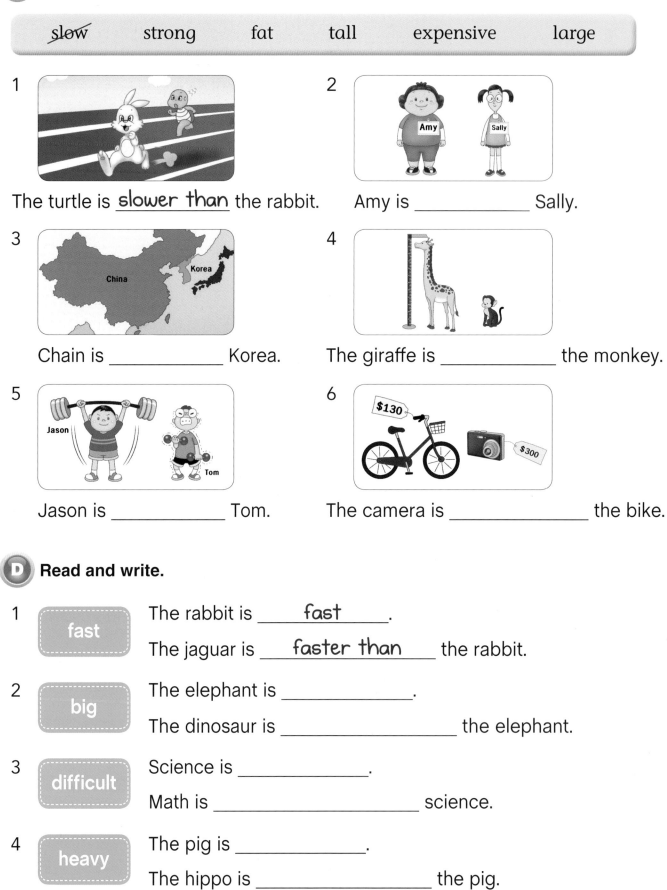

1
The turtle is __slower than__ the rabbit.

2
Amy is _____ Sally.

3
Chain is _____ Korea.

4
The giraffe is _____ the monkey.

5
Jason is _____ Tom.

6
The camera is _____ the bike.

D **Read and write.**

1 **fast**
The rabbit is _____fast_____.
The jaguar is ____faster than____ the rabbit.

2 **big**
The elephant is _____.
The dinosaur is _____ the elephant.

3 **difficult**
Science is _____.
Math is _____ science.

4 **heavy**
The pig is _____.
The hippo is _____ the pig.

READING GRAMMAR

A Read and write.

I Am Faster Than You

I am _____ than you.
pretty

I am _____ than you.
tall

I am _____ than you.
fast

I don't think so. Let's have a race.

You are _____ than me.
slow

Yes. You are _____ than me.
fast

B Look and write.

1
I am _____ _____ you.

2
I am _____ _____ you.

3
I am _____ _____ you.

4
You are _____ _____ me.

UNIT
18

Superlatives

GRAMMAR POINT

🔍 Let's Learn

+ -est	long ➡ longest, fast ➡ fastest, short ➡ shortest
+ -st	large ➡ largest, nice ➡ nicest, cute ➡ cutest
y ➡ i + -est	pretty ➡ prettiest, happy ➡ happiest, easy ➡ easiest
double consonant + -est	big ➡ biggest, hot ➡ hottest, fat ➡ fattest
most + adjective	beautiful ➡ most beautiful, expensive ➡ most expensive, difficult ➡ most difficult

🎤 Let's Say

Winter is the coldest season.

Tom is the tallest student.

The elephant is the largest animal.

The hippo is the heaviest animal.

Math is the most difficult class.

Cinderella is the most beautiful woman.

PRACTICE

A Read and write.

| cold | easy | tall | dirty | expensive | beautiful |
| pretty | fast | short | happy | difficult | interesting |

+ -est	y → i + -est	most + adjective
coldest	_____	_____
_____	_____	_____
_____	_____	_____
_____	_____	_____

B Look and write.

1

tall / short

The giraffe is _____the tallest_____ animal.
The monkey is _____the shortest_____ animal.

2
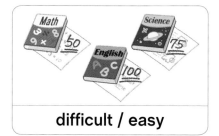
difficult / easy

Math is _____ class.
English is _____ class.

3

hot / cold

Summer is _____ season.
Winter is _____ season.

C **Look and write.**

| hot / cold | long / short | easy / difficult | dirty / clean | strong / weak | large / small |

1

Summer is ___the hottest___ season.
Winter is ___the coldest___ season.

2

Buster   Maxie   Cony

Buster is _____ dog.
Cony is _____ dog.

3

Mark   Jason   Tom

Jason is _____ boy
Tom is _____ boy.

4

The green snake is _____ animal.
The yellow snake is _____ animal.

5

The blouse is _____ clothes.
The pants are _____ clothes.

6

Math   English   Science

English is _____ class.
Math is _____ class.

D **Read and write.**

1 long / river → The Nile is ___the longest river___.

2 fast / animal → The cheetah is _____.

3 heavy / animal → The blue whale is _____.

4 high / mountain → Mt. Everest is _____.

5 cold / place → Antarctica is _____.

READING GRAMMAR

 Read and write.

Riddle Game

 What is _____ animal in the world?
heavy

 It's the blue whale.

 What is _____ mountain in the world?
high

 Mt. Everest.

 What is _____ place in the world?
cold

 It's Antarctica.

 Cool. Then what is _____ word
long

in the world?

 Well... I don't know.

 It's smile. It has a mile in it.

 Read and write.

1 The blue whale is _____ in the world.

2 Mt. Everest is _____ in the world.

3 Antarctica is _____ in the world.

4 "Smile" is _____ in the world.

Imperatives / Let's

GRAMMAR PoINT

🔍 Let's Learn

Imperatives		Let's
Do (Affirmative)	**Don't (Negative)**	
Wash your hands. Clean your room. Turn on the radio.	Don't play the piano. Don't close the window. Don't bring your umbrella.	Let's study English. Let's make a circle. Let's play baseball.

🎤 Let's Say

Close the window.

Turn off the light.

Wash your hands.

Don't bring your umbrella.

Don't eat junk food.

Don't open the door.

Let's make a snowman.

Let's play basketball.

Let's make a circle.

PRACTICE

A **Read and circle.**

1 (Brush) I Brushes your teeth.

2 Turns I Turn on the light.

3 Don't I Doesn't close the door.

4 Doesn't I Don't watch TV.

5 Don't touch I Touches your nose.

6 Doesn't bring I Bring your Jacket.

7 Do I Does your homework.

8 Eats I Don't eat junk food.

B **Look and write.**

~~sit~~   open   wash   bring   turn   play

____Don't sit____ on the bench.

_____ off the TV.

_____ the piano.

_____ the window.

_____ your hands.

_____ your umbrella.

C **Read, choose, and write.**

1
Your room is messy.
<u>Clean your room.</u>

2
The baby is sleeping.
_____

3
You have a cold.
_____

4
Your hands are dirty.
_____

5
The witch is outside.
_____

Don't play outside.

Be quiet, please.

Don't open the door.

Clean ~~your~~ room.

Wash your hands.

D **Read, look, and unscramble.**

1 It is sunny.

<u>Let's play basketball</u> . (basketball / play / Let's)

2 It is snowing.

_____ . (make / Let's / a snowman)

3 It is dark.

_____ . (Let's / the light / turn on)

4 Our faces are dirty.

_____ . (our faces / Let's / wash)

READING GRAMMAR

A Read and write.

School Rules

😊 **To Do**

_____ quiet in class.

_____ to your teachers.

_____ your school uniform.

_____ your hand to talk.

_____ your classmates.

☹ **Not To Do**

_____ _____ late for school.

_____ _____ in the hallway.

_____ _____ gum.

_____ _____ your cell phone.

_____ _____ trash.

run	listen	chew	be	help
wear	use	raise	throw	be

B Look and write.

1

_____

2

_____

3

_____

4

_____

UNIT 20

Can/May/Should

GRAMMAR POINT

🔍 Let's Learn

Can **Ability**	I can dance. / I can't swim. Can you dance? Yes, I can. / No, I can't.
Can / May **Permission**	You can (may) watch TV. / You can't (may not) sit down. Can (May) I come in? Yes, you can (may). / No, you can't (may not).
Should **Advice**	You should brush your teeth. You shouldn't watch TV.

🎙 Let's Say

The frog can jump.
It can't fly.

Can Lisa speak English?
No, she can't.

Can I borrow your book?
Yes, you can.

May I sit down?
No, you may not.

You should do your homework.

You shouldn't be late for school.

PRACTICE

A Read and circle.

1 He can (speak) / speaks English.

2 May I sits / sit down?

3 You may not comes / come in.

4 You should goes / go to bed.

5 Can I play / plays the violin?

6 You shouldn't watches / watch TV.

7 May I goes / go out?

8 You may use / uses my pen.

9 The frog can't fly / flies .

10 You can opens / open the door.

B Look and write.

1 May I open the window?
Yes, __you__ __may__.

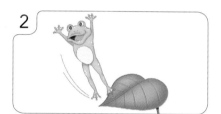

2 Can the frog jump high?
Yes, _____ _____.

3 May I play the piano?
No, _____ _____.

4 Can Lisa speak English?
No, _____ _____.

5 Can I borrow your book?
Yes, _____ _____.

6 Can I turn off the light?
No, _____ _____.

C **Read, match, and write** *should* **or** *shouldn't*.

1 She has a cold.

2 His room is dirty.

3 He is fat.

4 You look tired.

5 The baby is sleeping.

6 We don't do our homework.

7 It is cold outside.

He _____ eat junk food.

You _____ take a rest.

He _____ clean his room.

You _____ wear a jacket.

You _____ be quiet.

We _____ watch TV.

She __should__ go to a doctor.

D **Look and write.**

| can | can't | may | may not | should | shouldn't |

1
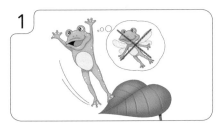

The frog __can__ jump high.

But it __can't__ fly.

2

_____ I sit on the bench?

No, you _____. It is wet.

3

_____ the monkeys climb the trees?

Yes, they _____.

4

We _____ sleep in class.

We _____ listen to the teacher.

READING GRAMMAR

A Read and write.

I Shouldn't Tell a Lie

B Read and correct.

1 May I goes out and play? → _____

2 You should finishes your homework. → _____

3 May I in-line skate? <u>Yes, you can.</u> → _____

4 <u>May you in-line skate?</u> Yes, I can → _____

A Look and write.

1

tall / short

The giraffe is ___taller than___ the kangroo.

The kangroo is ___shorter than___ the giraffe.

2

expensive / cheap

The camera is _____ the MP3 player.

The MP3 player is _____ the camera.

3

Amy   Lisa

fat / thin

Amy is _____ Lisa.

Lisa is _____ Amy.

4

Science English
75   100

difficult / easy

Science is _____ English.

English is _____ science.

B Read and write.

1 The cheetah / fast / animal → The cheetah is the fastest animal.

2 Summer / hot / season → _____

3 Skiing / interesting / sport → _____

4 The Nile / long / river → _____

5 Mt. Everest / high / moutain → _____

C Unscramble and match.

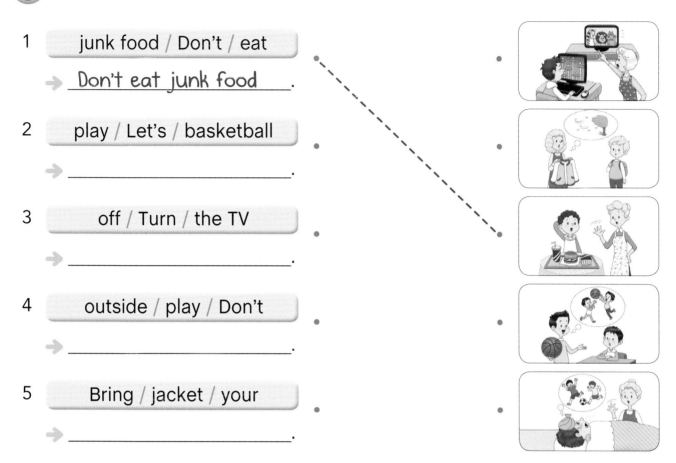

1 junk food / Don't / eat

→ _Don't eat junk food_ .

2 play / Let's / basketball

→ _____ .

3 off / Turn / the TV

→ _____ .

4 outside / play / Don't

→ _____ .

5 Bring / jacket / your

→ _____ .

D Read, match, and write.

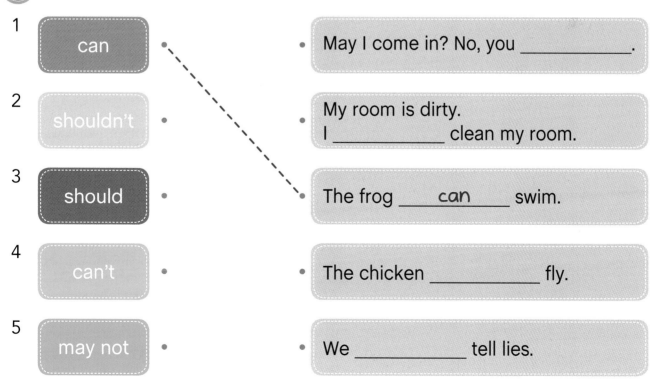

1 can

2 shouldn't

3 should

4 can't

5 may not

May I come in? No, you _____ .

My room is dirty.
I _____ clean my room.

The frog ____can____ swim.

The chicken _____ fly.

We _____ tell lies.

21 Prepositions of Place

GRAMMAR POINT

🔍 Let's Learn

in	on	under
in front of	behind	next to

🎤 Let's Say

The ball is in the box.

The bear is on the ball.

The slippers are under the bed.

Where is the car?
It is in front of the house.

Where are the rabbits?
They are behind the tree.

Where is the clock?
It is next to the TV.

96

PRACTICE

A Look and mark O or X.

1    X   The lamp is behind the bed.

2    The girl is in front of the door.

3    The socks are on the sofa.

4    The bear is next to the ball.

B Look, circle, and write.

1

The clock is _____ next to _____ the TV.
(in / on / next to)

2

The chairs are _____ the table.
(on / behind / under)

3

The slippers are _____ the bed.
(in / under / next to)

4

The car is _____ the house.
(in front of / behind / in)

5

The fish are _____ the fish tank.
(in front of / in / under)

 **Look and write.**

Where is the rabbit?

It is _____in_____ the hat.

It is _____ the hat.

It is _____ the hat.

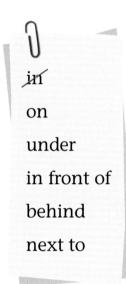

~~in~~

on

under

in front of

behind

next to

Where are the rabbits?

They are _____ the tree.

They are _____ the tree.

They are _____ the tree.

 **Look and write.**

1

Where __is__ the girl?
She is __in front of__ the door.

2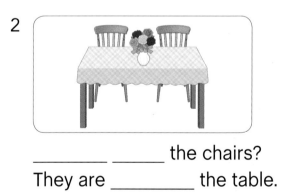

_____ _____ the chairs?
They are _____ the table.

3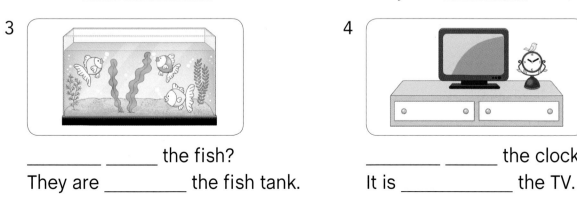

_____ _____ the fish?
They are _____ the fish tank.

4

_____ _____ the clock?
It is _____ the TV.

READING GRAMMAR

A **Read and write.**

Hide and Seek

The baby animals are playing hide and seek.

The puppy is
_____ the swing.

The kittens are
_____ the seesaw.

The piglet is
_____ the jungle gym.

The ducklings are
_____ the slide.

The chicks are
_____ the trees.

"Hey, babies. Time to go home," their mothers say.
"Okay, Mom!" They go home.

B **Read and write.**

1 _____ _____ the puppy? It is _____ the swing.

2 _____ _____ the kittens? They are _____ the seesaw.

3 _____ _____ the piglet? It is _____ the jungle gym.

4 _____ _____ the ducklings? They are _____ the slide.

5 _____ _____ the chicks? They are _____ the trees.

Prepositions of Time

GRAMMAR POINT

🔍 Let's Learn

at + time	on + day / date	in + month / season
at 4 o'clock at 7:30 at noon	on Monday on Sundays on May 5	in July in winter in the morning

🎤 Let's Say

I get up at 7 o'clock.

We have lunch at noon.

It is snowy in winter.

Tom's birthday is on Monday.

Halloween is in October.

The Christmas party is on December 24.

When is your birthday? It is on September 18.

When is your vacation? It is in August.

When is lunchtime? It is at noon.

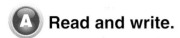

PRACTICE

A Read and write.

3 o'clock	spring	7:30	night	Mondays
the evening	Saturday	June 2	December

at	on	in
3 o'clock	_____	_____
_____	_____	_____
_____	_____	_____

B Look, circle, and write.

1

I get up _____at_____ 7 o'clock.
(at)/ on / in

2

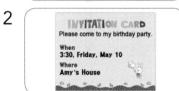

Amy's birthday is _____ May.
(at / on / in)

3

It is hot _____ summer.
(at / on / in)

4

She goes to an art class _____ Friday.
(at / on / in)

5

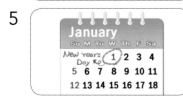

New Year's Day is _____ January 1.
(at / on / in)

C Look and write *at*, *on*, or *in*.

1

When is Halloween?
It is __in__ October.
It is _____ October 31.
It is _____ Thursday.

2

When is Amy's birthday party?
It is _____ May.
It is _____ May 10.
It is _____ Friday.
It is _____ 3:30.

3

When is the Christmas party?
It is _____ December.
It is _____ December 24.
It is _____ Tuesday.
It is _____ 8 o'clock.

D Read and write *at*, *on*, or *in*.

 When is Jimmy's birthday party?

 It is __in__ June. It is _____ June 22.

 Let me see the calendar. It is _____ Saturday.

 What time does the party start?

 It starts _____ 1 o'clock. Let's go together.

 Oh, I'm sorry. I have to see the dentist _____ the afternoon.

READING GRAMMAR

A **Read and write *at*, *on*, or *in*.**

Dear Kelly,

Please come to my birthday party.
It is _____ August 10. It is _____ Saturday.
The party begins _____ 2 o'clock.
My birthday is _____ summer, so we can play in the pool.
See you then.

Your friend,
Andy

Dear Andy,

Thanks for inviting me to your birthday party.
Sorry, but I have an appointment _____ August 10.
I have to see the dentist _____ 2:30.
And I have to visit my grandma _____ the evening.
Have fun.

Your friend,
Kelly

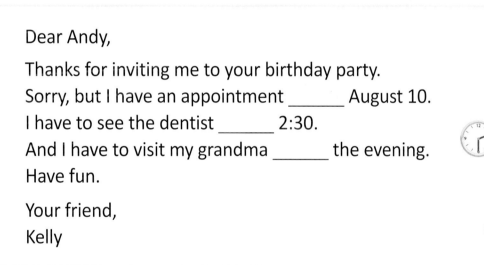

B **Look and write.**

1
When is Andy's birthday party?
It is _____ summer. It is _____ August 10.
It is _____ Saturday. It starts _____ 2 o'clock.

2
Kelly has an appointment _____ August 10.
She has to see the dentist _____ 2:30.
She has to visit her grandma _____ the evening.

UNIT 23

There Is / There Isn't / Is There…?

GRAMMAR POINT

🔍 Let's Learn

	Countable Noun	Uncountable Noun
Affirmative	There is an apple. There are two apples. There are some apples.	There is some milk.
Negative	There isn't an apple. There aren't any apples.	There isn't any milk.
Question	Is there an apple? Yes, there is. / No, there isn't. Are there any apples? Yes, there are. / No, there aren't.	Is there any milk? Yes, there is. / No, there isn't.

🎙 Let's Say

There is a pencil case.
There are two notebooks.
There are some pencils.
There aren't any erasers.
Are there any books? Yes, there are.

There is some bread.
There is some milk.
There isn't any juice.
Is there any jam? Yes, there is.
Is there any butter? No, there isn't.

PRACTICE

A **Read and circle.**

1 There is l (are) some cookies.   2 There is l are a kangaroo.

3 There is l are some cheese.   4 There is l are three puppies.

5 There is l are some watches.   6 There isn't l aren't any money.

7 There isn't l aren't any eggs.   8 There isn't l aren't an orange.

9 There isn't l aren't any bread.   10 There isn't l aren't a flower.

B **Choose and write.**

There is	There are	There isn't	There aren't

1

___There is___ an elephant.

2

_____ some fish.

3

_____ any chairs.

4

_____ some salt.

5

_____ a cake.

6

_____ any bread.

C Look and write the answer.

1

Is there any money?

_____No, there isn't._____

2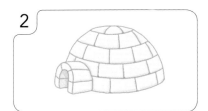

Is there an igloo?

_____

3

Is there any butter?

_____

4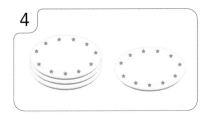

Are there any dishes?

_____

5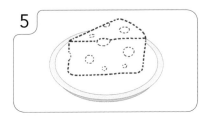

Is there any cheese?

_____

6

Are there any chairs?

_____

D Look and write.

1 ___There is___ a cake.

2 _____ any cookies.

3 _____ some orange juice.

4 _____ some peaches.

5 _____ a watermelon?

Yes, _____.

6 _____ any bread?

No, _____.

7 _____ any candies?

No, _____.

8 _____ any milk?

Yes, _____.

READING GRAMMAR

A Read and write.

There Aren't Any Cookies

"Oh, I'm hungry," Jake said.

"____ _____ any cookies?" Jake asked.

"Yes, _____ ____," Mom answered.

"No, _____ _____ any cookies," Jake said.

"Then _____ ____ some bread," Mom said.

"No, _____ _____ any bread," Jake said.

"_____ ____ a hole in the wall.

Oh, _____ _____ some cookies.

_____ ____ some bread, too.

Those mice have my cookies and bread!"

Jake cried out.

B Read and correct.

1 Is there any cookies? ➡ _____

2 There isn't any cookies. ➡ _____

3 There aren't any bread. ➡ _____

4 There are some bread. ➡ _____

What ...! How ...!

GRAMMAR POINT

🔍 Let's Learn

Exclamations		
What + a / an + adjective + noun + (S + V)!	What + adjective + plural noun + (S + V)!	How + adjective + (S + V)!
What a nice hat (it is)! What a beautiful girl (she is)! What an ugly boy (he is)!	What pretty flowers (they are)! What tall boys (they are)! What big houses (they are)!	How expensive (it is)! How smart (she is)! How sweet (they are)!

🎤 Let's Say

What a beautiful flower
(it is)!

What a tall girl
(she is)!

What tall buildings
(they are)!

What strong boys
(they are)!

How fast
(it is)!

How expensive
(they are)!

PRACTICE

A **Read and check the exclamations.**

1 ☐ What is it?   ✓ What a nice hat!

2 ☐ What a wonderful day!   ☐ What day is it?

3 ☐ What tall boys!   ☐ What are they doing?

4 ☐ How are you?   ☐ How beautiful!

5 ☐ How old are you?   ☐ How old it is!

6 ☐ How lovely!   ☐ How is he?

B **Look and write *What* or *How*.**

1  ___How___ smart they are!

2  _____ big hippos!

3  _____ strong they are!

4  _____ an ugly frog it is!

5 _____ a cute girl she is!

C Look and write.

What	How

strong	dirty	pretty	big	~~tall~~	fast

1. ___How___ ___tall___ she is!

2. _____ _____ they are!

3. _____ _____ hippos!

4. _____ a _____ airplane!

5. _____ _____ they are!

6. _____ a _____ flower!

D Read and unscramble.

1. | flower! | | What | | beautiful | | a |

   → ___What a beautiful flower!___

2. | ugly | | an | | What | | frog! |

   → _____

3. | they are! | | tall | | buildings | | What |

   → _____

4. | is! | | fast | | How | | it |

   → _____

5. | are! | | How | | they | | sweet |

   → _____

READING GRAMMAR

A Read and write.

What Dirty Socks!

_____ a _____ boy he is!

_____ _____ he is!

_____ _____ he is!

_____ _____ socks they are!

| What   How | | smart   dirty   tall   handsome |

B Look and write.

1 _____ ___ _____ boy he is!

2 _____ _____ he is!

3 _____ _____ he is!

4 _____ _____ socks they are!

Review VI — Units 21-24

A Look, read, and write.

1 The teddy bear is _on_ the bed.

2 The toys are _____ the box.

3 The slippers are _____ the bed.

4 Where is the chair?

It is _____ the desk.

5 Where is the bat?

It is _____ the door.

6 Where are the glasses?

They are _____ the book.

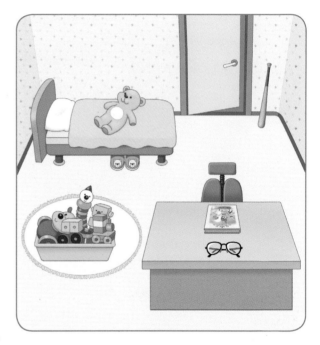

in front of	~~on~~	under	next to	behind	in

B Read and write.

1 She goes to sleep __at__ 9:30.

2 I have English class _____ Monday.

3 Susan's birthday is _____ June.

4 Don't play the violin _____ night.

5 They clean their house _____ Saturdays.

6 We can go skiing _____ winter.

7 Summer vacation starts _____ July 24.

at

in

on

C Look and write.

1
<u>There</u> <u>are</u> some watches.

2
_____ _____ an umbrella.

3
_____ _____ any pencils.

4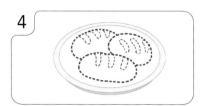
_____ _____ any bread.

5
Are there any candies?
No, _____ _____.

6
Is there any water?
Yes, _____ _____.

D Look and write *What* or *How*.

1
<u>What</u> a beautiful flower!

2
_____ cute she is!

3
_____ tall buildings!

4
_____ big they are!

GRAMMAR SUMMARY

 ## Regular Plural Nouns

Regular Plural Nouns			
+ -s	+ -es	f, fe ➡ v + -es	consonant + y ➡ i + -es
an apple ➡ apples a book ➡ books a cat ➡ cats a toy ➡ toys	a bus ➡ buses a fox ➡ foxes a dish ➡ dishes a peach ➡ peaches	a leaf ➡ leaves a wolf ➡ wolves a scarf ➡ scarves a knife ➡ knives	a puppy ➡ puppies a baby ➡ babies a candy ➡ candies a butterfly ➡ butterflies

 ## Possessive Adjectives

Subject Pronouns		Possessive Adjectives	
I	my	This is my toy.	/ My toy is red.
you	your	This is your toy.	/ Your toy is red.
he	his	This is his toy.	/ His toy is red.
she	her	This is her toy.	/ Her toy is red.
it	its	This is its toy.	/ Its toy is red.
we	our	This is our toy.	/ Our toy is red.
they	their	This is their toy.	/ Their toy is red.
Amy	Amy's	This is Amy's toy.	/ Amy's toy is red.

 ## Possessive Pronouns

Possessive Adjectives		Possessive Pronouns	
my	mine	This is my pen.	= This pen is mine.
your	yours	This is your pen.	= This pen is yours.
his	his	This is his pen.	= This pen is his.
her	hers	This is her pen.	= This pen is hers.
our	ours	This is our pen.	= This pen is ours.
their	theirs	This is their pen.	= This pen is theirs.
Amy	Amy's	This is Amy's pen.	= This pen is Amy's.

Present Simple

Present Simple (Affirmatives)			
I You We They	drink milk.	He She It Jane	drinks milk.

	Regular Verbs	Irregular Verbs
+ -s	drink ➡ drinks, play ➡ plays	have ➡ has
+ -es	watch ➡ watches, brush ➡ brushes	go ➡ goes
y ➡ i + -es	study ➡ studies, cry ➡ cries	do ➡ does

 Present Continuous

Present Continuous (Affirmatives)		
I	am	sleeping.
You	are	sleeping.
He / She / It	is	sleeping.
We / You / They	are	sleeping.

+ -ing	**e + -ing**	**double consonant + -ing**
play ➡ playing sing ➡ singing walk ➡ walking	make ➡ making dance ➡ dancing drive ➡ driving	run ➡ running swim ➡ swimming hit ➡ hitting

 Comparatives

+ -er	long ➡ longer, fast ➡ faster, short ➡ shorter
+ -r	large ➡ larger, nice ➡ nicer, cute ➡ cuter
y ➡ i + -er	pretty ➡ prettier, happy ➡ happier, easy ➡ easier
double consonant + -er	big ➡ bigger, hot ➡ hotter, fat ➡ fatter
more + adjective	beautiful ➡ more beautiful, expensive ➡ more expensive, difficult ➡ more difficult

Superlatives

+ -est	long ➡ longest, fast ➡ fastest, short ➡ shortest
+ -st	large ➡ largest, nice ➡ nicest, cute ➡ cutest
y ➡ i + -est	pretty ➡ prettiest, happy ➡ happiest, easy ➡ easiest
double consonant + -est	big ➡ biggest, hot ➡ hottest, fat ➡ fattest
most + adjective	beautiful ➡ most beautiful, expensive ➡ most expensive, difficult ➡ most difficult

Can / May / Should

Can Ability	I can dance. / I can't swim. Can you dance? Yes, I can. / No, I can't.
Can / May Permission	You can (may) watch TV. / You can't (may not) sit down. Can (May) I come in? Yes, you can (may). / No, you can't (may not).
Should Advice	You should brush your teeth. You shouldn't watch TV.

Prepositions of Place

in	on	under

in front of	behind	next to

Prepositions of Time

at + time	on + day / date	in + month / season
at 4 o'clock at 7:30 at noon	on Monday on Sundays on May 5	in July in winter in the morning